Text and Illustrations Copyright © 2017 by A.C. Steele.
Address all inquiries to:
Email: steeleac4@gmail.com

ISBN-13:
978-1947045194 (Baobab Publishing)

ISBN-10:
1947045199

Author's Bio

Tamika Steele is a professional wife and mother of two lovely little girls. She grew up as a child of military parents and thus had to travel a lot for a while. Still making new friends, during those times she learned to always be true to herself no matter who else was around. Tamika is trying to impart that same quality to her young daughters who will also have many experiences in life but must always know who and whose they are. Tamika wrote this book for her daughters and other girls like them, after realizing that so many young girls forget that there can never be a more beautiful them than the one they are and that *they have a purpose*.

Dedication

"First, thank God for inspiring me to write this book. This book is dedicated to my two beautiful daughters (my very own beloved brown girls) who were the inspiration for this book and to every single brown girl in the world. Keep shining and always remember you are beautifully and wonderfully made.

Much love ❤!"

Tamika

This Book Belongs To a Beloved
Beautiful Princess
Named

_____

I know my worth no matter my color.

I am just as valuable as any other.

Dark, almond, chocolate or light,

In any shade of brown I am just right.

Tall, skinny, short or small,

I have been a princess
since the day I was called.

Curly, straight, braided or puffs,

I am beautiful
and I will always be enough

Because I am a beloved brown girl as happy as can be

and I am happy just being me.

Can you imagine how boring the world would seem without beautiful brown girls like me splashed in between?

We are strong, educated, intelligent girls

and we have been strategically placed
all around the world.

We are royalty in all shades of brown and are all princesses adorned with a crown.

I am a beloved brown girl through and through and to me, I will always be true.

So I will continue to embrace and love me

and will be the best beautiful
beloved brown girl that I can be.

Discussion Questions:

What do you hope to be when you grow up?

_____

What are your favorite things to do?

_____

What makes you laugh/smile?

_____

What do you think beautiful means?

_____

51991077R00017

Made in the USA
Lexington, KY
07 September 2019